Good Question!

How Is My Brain Like a Supercomputer?
AND OTHER QUESTIONS ABOUT . . .
The Human Body

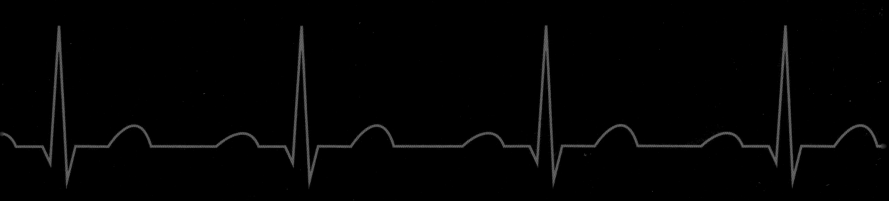

STERLING CHILDREN'S BOOKS
New York

🌰

STERLING CHILDREN'S BOOKS
New York

An Imprint of Sterling Publishing
387 Park Avenue South
New York, NY 10016

Photo credits: 5: © Robert Churchill/iStockphoto; 6: © Jezperklauzen/iStockphoto; 9 © Michelle Gibson/iStockphoto;
10: © Professor Terry Allen/Science Photo Library/Corbis; 17: © Aleksei Lazukov/Shutterstock; 18, 21: © Christopher Futcher/
iStockphoto; 26: © cosmin4000/iStockphoto/Thinkstock

ISBN 978-1-4549-0680-3 [hardcover]
ISBN 978-1-4549-0681-0 [paperback]

Library of Congress Cataloging-in-Publication Data

Stewart, Melissa, author.
    How is my brain like a supercomputer? : and other questions about the human body / Melissa Stewart ;
illustrated by Peter Bull.
        pages cm. -- (Good question)
    Audience: 6 & up.
    Audience: K to grade 3.
      ISBN 978-1-4549-0680-3 (hardback) -- ISBN 978-1-4549-0681-0 (paperback)
    1. Human physiology--Miscellanea--Juvenile literature. I. Bull, Peter, 1960- illustrator. II. Title.
QP37.S757 2014
612--dc23
                                                                          2014000919

Distributed in Canada by Sterling Publishing
c/o Canadian Manda Group, 165 Dufferin Street
Toronto, Ontario, Canada M6K 3H6
Distributed in the United Kingdom by GMC Distribution Services
Castle Place, 166 High Street, Lewes, East Sussex, England BN7 1XU
Distributed in Australia by Capricorn Link (Australia) Pty. Ltd.
P.O. Box 704, Windsor, NSW 2756, Australia

Design by Andrea Miller
Art by Peter Bull

For information about custom editions, special sales, and premium and corporate purchases, please contact Sterling Special
Sales at 800-805-5489 or specialsales@sterlingpublishing.com.

Manufactured in China
Lot #:
2 4 6 8 10 9 7 5 3 1
04/14

www.sterlingpublishing.com/kids

CONTENTS

Why am I different from everyone else on Earth?

More than 7 billion people are alive right now, but none of them is just like you. Your parents might have the same color hair or eyes. If you have brothers or sisters, their chins or noses might be shaped like yours. But no two faces are exactly the same.

Some people might speak like you, but no two voices sound exactly alike. And no one has the same feelings and ideas as you. You are special, and so is every bit of your body—from the tip of your nose to the bottoms of your toes.

Why is your body unique? To find out, you'll need to take a close-up look at what your body is made of. In fact, you'll need a microscope.

Right now, your body is made of about 100,000,000,000,000 tiny cells. But when your life began, you were made of just one cell. That cell had a set of instructions called deoxyribonucleic acid, or DNA. DNA makes you the special person you are. Unless you have an identical twin brother or sister, no one in the world has the same exact set of DNA instructions as you.

From our skin, eyes, and hair to the way we act and think, we are all unique.

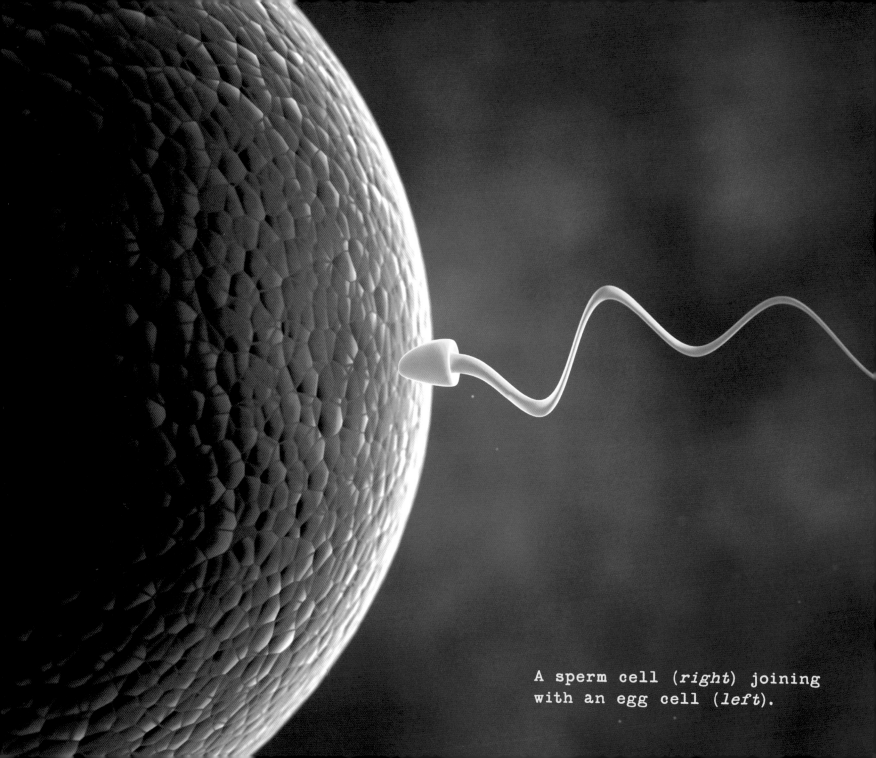

A sperm cell (*right*) joining with an egg cell (*left*).

How does my DNA make me special?

DNA is like a collection of recipes. Each "recipe" in DNA is called a gene. A gene has step-by-step instructions for making one kind of protein. Proteins determine what you look like and they keep your body working.

Every cell in your body has the same exact collection of recipes, but each cell uses only a few of them. When a cell is running low on an important protein, its gene recipe gets turned on and the cell starts to produce more copies of that protein.

The mixture of proteins in your cells controls the color of your hair and eyes. Proteins also determine the shape of your nose. And they affect how fast you can run and how tall you'll grow. That's why your DNA instructions make you who you are.

Where do my genes come from?

When a tiny sperm cell from your dad joined with an egg cell from your mom, your first cell was created. About half the material in that cell came from your dad. The other half came from your mom. You probably look a little bit like your mom because some of your genes came from her. And you probably look like your dad in other ways because some of your genes came from him.

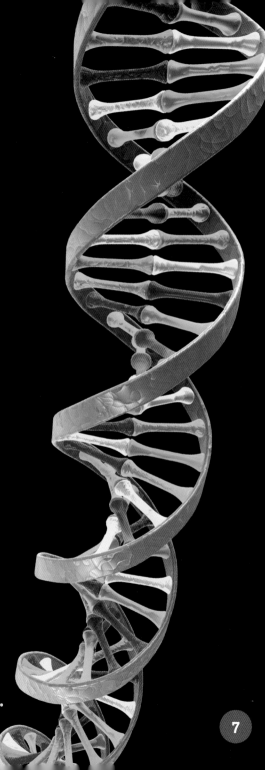

DNA looks like a spiraling ladder.
This structure is called a double helix.

How did I grow into a baby?

Your first cell started to grow right away. After about 30 hours, it split in half to form two cells. Then those cells grew and they split, too. Four cells. Sixteen cells. Sixty-four cells. Over and over, your cells grew and split and multiplied. Soon there were enough cells to form a ball.

After about a week, your growing ball of cells attached to your mother's body. By then, your DNA was already directing your cells to separate into three groups. One group became your skin, brain, and nerves. The second group became your muscles, bones, and blood. And the third group became your stomach, lungs, and intestines.

After only ten weeks, many important parts of your tiny body had already formed. You had arms and legs, fingers and toes, ears and eyes. And with special equipment, your parents, doctors, and nurses could see all of those parts. You kept on growing and developing for about seven more months. Then, finally, you were born.

Why do I have a belly button?

While you were inside your mom's body, you couldn't breathe air or eat food. The oxygen and nutrients you needed to survive came from your mom through a tube called the umbilical cord. The umbilical cord, which was attached to your belly, also carried wastes out of your body.

When you were born, your umbilical cord was cut. After a few weeks, the last little bit of the cord dried out and fell off, leaving behind your belly button. Most belly buttons are sunken in, but some stick out a little bit. We aren't sure why some belly buttons are "innies" and others are "outies."

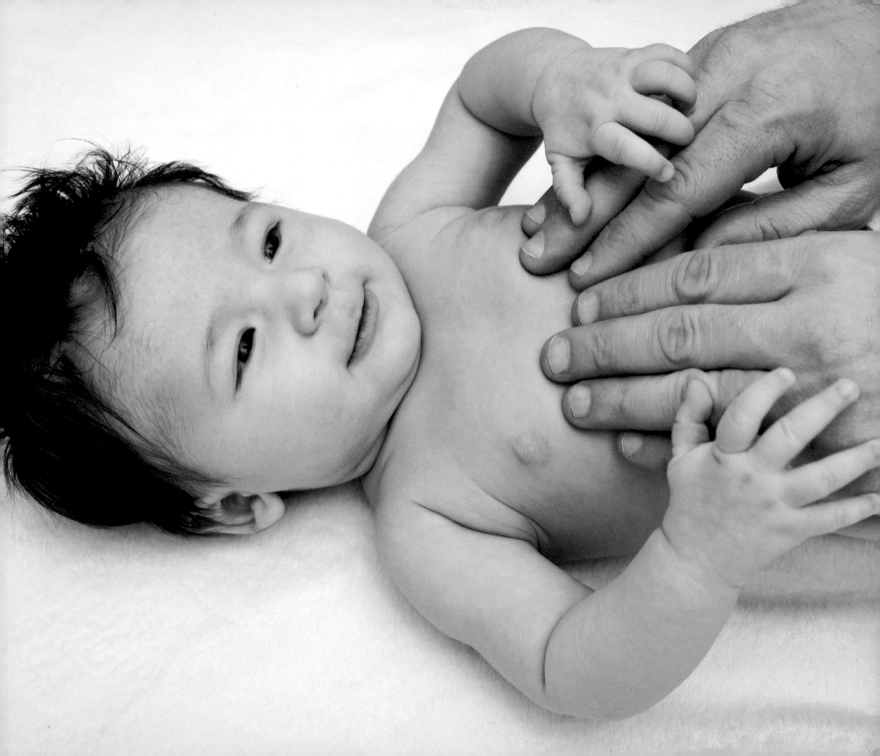

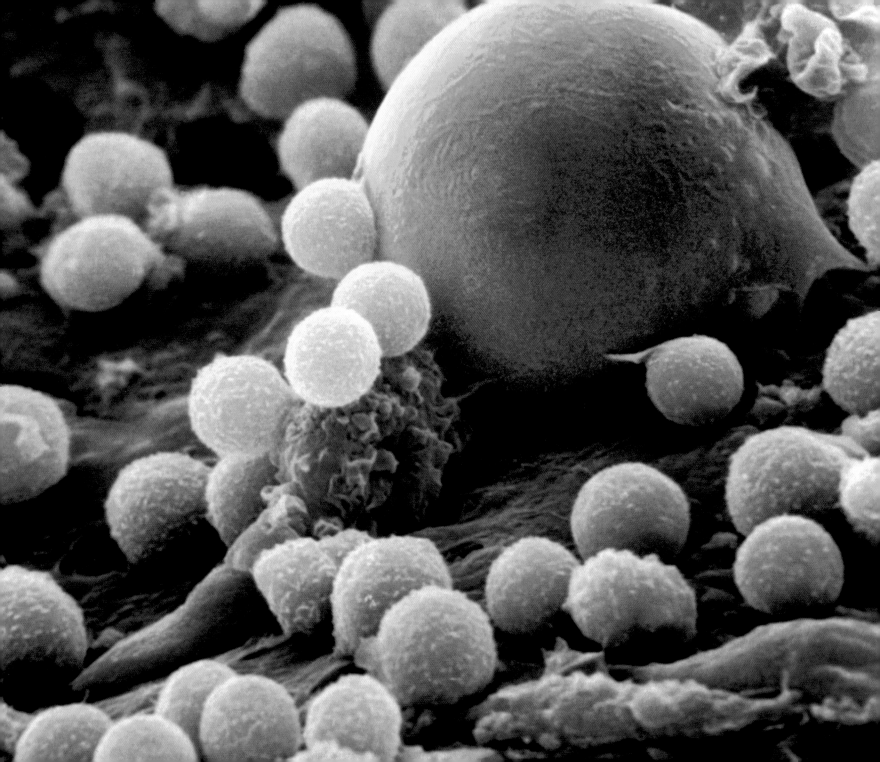

Are all the cells in my body the same?

Some of your cells look like blobs of jelly. Others are shaped like ice cubes. Why do your cells come in so many shapes and sizes? Because they have lots of different jobs to do. Thin, flat skin cells overlap to protect the inside of your body the way shingles on a roof protect a house. Big, round adipose cells are full of fat. Muscle cells are stretchy, so they can help you move.

Your DNA recipe collection has instructions for making about 25,000 kinds of proteins. Those proteins combine in different ways to make more than 200 kinds of cells.

What happens when cells work together?

Most of the cells in your body are part of a team. That team is called a tissue. The cells in a tissue work together to do a job. Nerve cells form nervous tissue. Some nervous tissue sends messages from your brain to your muscles, so they know when to move.

Groups of tissues work together, too. They form organs. Your stomach is an organ that breaks down food. Your heart is an organ that pumps blood.

Most organs are part of a larger body system. Your circulatory system includes your heart plus all the blood vessels that carry blood to every single cell in your body. Other major body systems digest food, help you breathe, and fight diseases.

This photograph was taken though a microscope. It shows a round adipose cell (*pink*) and two kinds of germ-fighting white blood cells (*yellow, purple*).

What is my biggest and heaviest organ?

It's not your heart or your brain or your lungs. It's your skin. That's right! Your skin is a single organ that covers your entire body! In most places, your skin isn't much thicker than a nickel, but you couldn't live without it. Your skin's top layer, or epidermis, protects the rest of your body from the outside world. It keeps out wind and water, dust and dirt. It also protects you from germs that could make you sick.

Your skin's middle layer, or dermis, is full of tiny structures that do all kinds of jobs. Touch sensors in your dermis help you sense the world around you. They tell you when it's time to put on a coat or get out of the sun. They also let you know when a spider is crawling up your arm or a pebble is in your shoe.

The hair growing out of your dermis helps keep you warm. And when your body heats up, the sweat glands in your dermis help you cool down. Sweat glands squeeze drops of watery sweat onto your skin. In no time at all, the liquid evaporates. It turns into a gas and rises into the air, taking the heat in your skin along for the ride.

Your skin's bottom layer, or hypodermis, stores fats. It releases some of those fats into your blood every time you need an extra boost of energy. The fats in your hyodermis also help to keep you warm, and they cushion your inner organs from knocks and bumps.

Human Skin

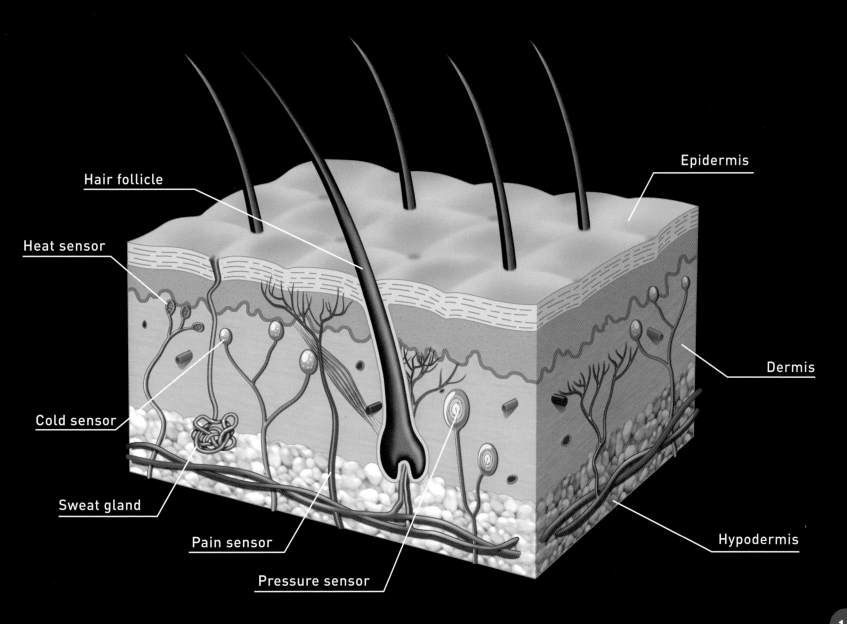

Hair follicle

Heat sensor

Cold sensor

Sweat gland

Pain sensor

Pressure sensor

Epidermis

Dermis

Hypodermis

Nervous System

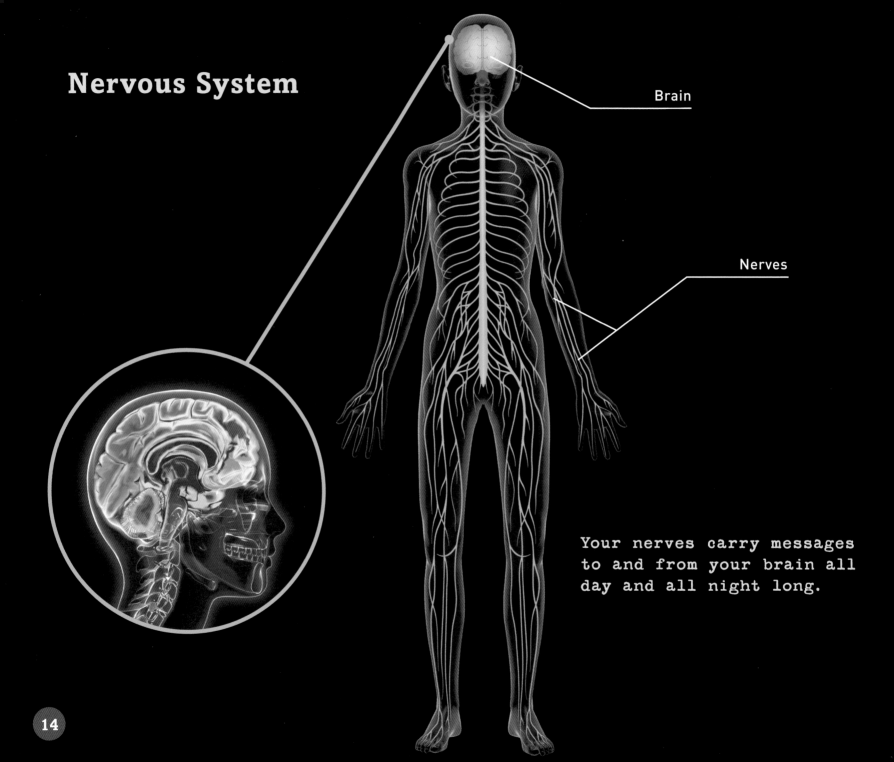

Brain

Nerves

Your nerves carry messages to and from your brain all day and all night long.

How is my brain like a supercomputer?

We use computers because they can collect, sort, and store information quickly. But no computer in the world is as fast or as powerful as your brain.

Your brain is your body's boss. From reading and writing to running a race, it controls everything you do. Your brain sends out about 6,000,000,000,000 messages every minute. And it can store up to 1,000,000,000,000,000,000,000,000 bits of information.

Think it takes a lot of energy to do all that work? You're right. Your brain uses up to 25 percent of all nutrients that come from your food. So if you want to think right, you need to eat right.

Your brain may be your body's boss, but it couldn't do its job without a whole lot of help from the miles and miles of nerves snaking through your body. Nerves carry millions of messages to and from your brain every second—even when you're asleep.

Messages traveling to your brain let you know what's happening inside and outside your body. Your eyes send messages about what you see. Your ears send messages about what you hear. Sensors in your nose, tongue, skin, and other organs send messages, too.

Your brain sorts through all the messages. Then it studies them and sends out its own messages. They tell different parts of your body how to react.

All these messages race through your body faster than you can blink an eye. And that makes it possible for you to dodge a ball, rap a rhyme, or laugh when your friend tells a joke.

How do my five senses help me understand the world?

Find a mirror and look closely at your face. You'll see some important body parts. Your eyes, ears, skin, nose, and tongue are all sensory organs. They help you sense, or understand, the world around you. Your five senses—seeing, hearing, touching, smelling, and tasting—play a role in your life every day. They can fill you with joy and they can protect you from danger.

When your eyes see a delicious dessert, you feel happy. But when they spot a bully, you turn and walk the other way. Your ears can hear the sound of laughter and the blare of a fire alarm.

Your skin can feel a hug or a hot stove. Your nose smells what's cooking in the school cafeteria, and when the janitor has just cleaned the restrooms. Your tongue can enjoy the yummy taste of homemade chocolate chip cookies. But it also lets you know when you're eating rotten food that could make you sick. Thank goodness for your five senses!

How many senses do you use when you peel an orange? More than you might think! While your eyes (sight) and fingers (touch) work together to remove the peel, your nose (smell) lets you know if the fruit is perfectly ripe.

Compact bone

Spongy bone

How many bones do I have?

When you were born, you had more than 300 bones in your body. Over the years, some of them have fused, or grown together. Different kids' bones fuse at different rates, so it's hard to say how many bones you have in your body right now. But when you're all grown up, you'll have 206 bones. More than half of them will be in your hands and feet.

It's hard to imagine what you'd look like if you didn't have bones. You'd be nothing more than a pile of skin and guts heaped on the floor. That's because your bones do more than help you move around. They support your body and give you shape. They also protect your most important organs. Your skull protects your brain. Your ribs protect your heart and lungs.

Even though bones are five times stronger than steel, they don't weigh very much. That's because most bones aren't solid. They are made of two kinds of tissue. Below the hard, dense compact bone on the outside is a softer layer called spongy bone. Spongy bone is full of tiny holes.

Why do bones break?

Most of the time, your bones have no trouble absorbing the pressure you put on them when you hit a baseball or jump out of a tree. Like a wooden pencil, bones are flexible. They can bend a little bit, especially if your brain lets them know what to expect. But if a car door suddenly slams into your finger or you fall off your bike and land on your wrist, the pressure might be more than your bones can take. Sometimes a bone cracks just a little bit. But it can also snap in half or shatter into several pieces.

Lots of kids break a bone or two falling off a bike, skating, or playing a sport. Luckily, young bones heal quickly. If you break a wrist, it will probably heal in three weeks. But your grandmother's or grandfather's broken wrist could take eight weeks to heal.

How do my muscles help me move?

Your body has more than 650 muscles. And you can't move without them.

How many muscles are you using right now? Probably more than you think. It takes twenty different muscles to smile and more than forty to frown. You use at least two hundred muscles to walk across the street. That's a whole lot of pulling power.

Muscles only move in one direction. They can pull, but they can't push. So that means many muscles come in pairs. For example, the biceps and triceps in your arm work together. When you want to bend your arm at the elbow, your biceps does the pulling. And when you want to straighten your arm, your triceps pulls in the opposite direction.

Do I control all my muscles?

Nope. You have three kinds of muscles in your body—skeletal, cardiac, and smooth. You use skeletal muscles to pick up a pencil, kick a soccer ball, and wiggle your nose. And before you do any of these things, you think about it. That's because you can control the movement of your skeletal muscles.

But you don't control the cardiac muscle in your heart or the smooth muscles that control organ functions inside your body. Think about it. When's the last time you decided it was time to breathe in air or pump blood or digest your food? You don't have to think about any of these life-or-death movements because your body controls the muscles all by itself.

Muscles in Action

Biceps pulling

Triceps

Biceps

Triceps pulling

Digestive System

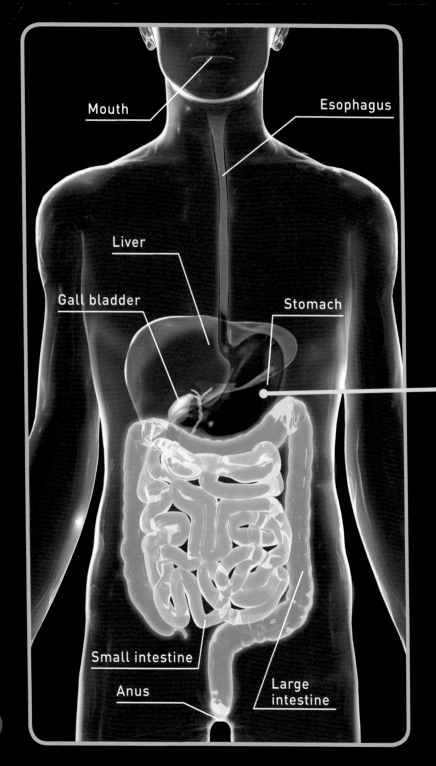

Mouth

Esophagus

Liver

Gall bladder

Stomach

Small intestine

Anus

Large intestine

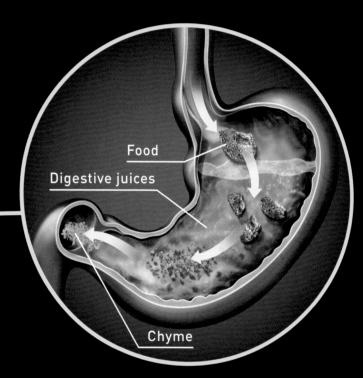

Food

Digestive juices

Chyme

What happens to the food I eat?

As you eat an apple, your mind focuses on its sweet flavor and crisp crunch. But after you swallow, you probably don't give that apple another thought. That's because smooth muscles in your esophagus take over. They push the chewed food down to your stomach.

Your stomach is a pouch that can stretch like a water balloon to hold lots of food. When your stomach is full, digestive juices flow in and more smooth muscles get to work. They spend about three hours mashing and mixing food into a thick, soupy mixture called chyme. That's when things start to get even more interesting.

Some of the useful nutrients from the apple move into your capillaries, tiny blood vessels that surround your stomach. The rest of the chyme enters your small intestine—a long, coiled tube below your stomach. After more digestive juices enter from your liver and gall bladder, the food continues to break down for about six hours. Then more nutrients pass into nearby capillaries.

Finally, the leftovers move into your large intestine. Then more smooth muscles squeeze water out of the chyme, leaving behind brown lumps of poop. After about a day of digestion, the remains of the apple will pass out of your body through your anus when you go to the bathroom.

How much air do I breathe in every day?

Most of the time, you inhale about 1.6 gallons (6 liters) of air a minute. That works out to 96 gallons (360 L) of air per hour and more than 2,300 gallons (8,600 L) per day. All that air enters your body through your mouth and nose. But you don't have to think about it. That's because smooth muscles inside your chest are hard at work—all day and all night, for as long as you live.

First, your diaphragm drops down, pulling air into your mouth and nose. Then your intercostal muscles lift your ribs up and out. As your chest expands, air rushes down a tube called the trachea. Finally, the air enters your lungs and fills them up like balloons.

What happens next? The oxygen in air moves into capillaries surrounding the tiny grape-shaped alveolar sacs deep inside your lungs. At the same time, a gas called carbon dioxide moves out of your blood and into your lungs.

As your diaphragm relaxes, it rises. Then your intercostal muscles push your ribs down and in. Your chest shrinks, and your lungs collapse like balloons losing air. The air in your lungs—and the carbon dioxide it contains—zips up through your trachea. And then, as you exhale, the air exits your body through your nose and mouth.

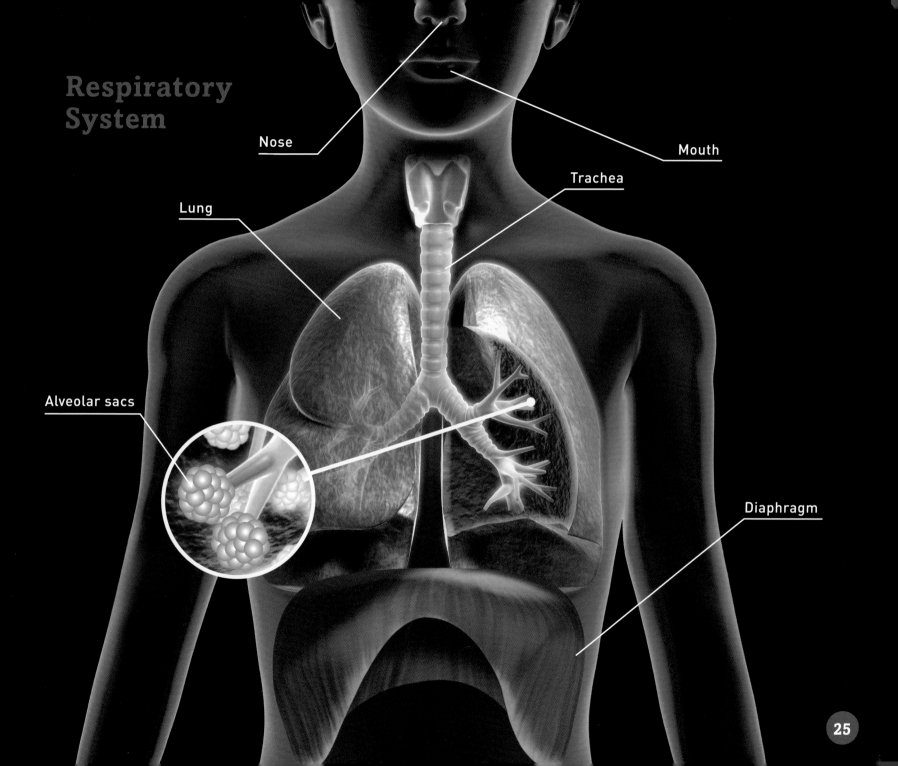

Respiratory System

Nose

Mouth

Trachea

Lung

Alveolar sacs

Diaphragm

25

Circulatory System

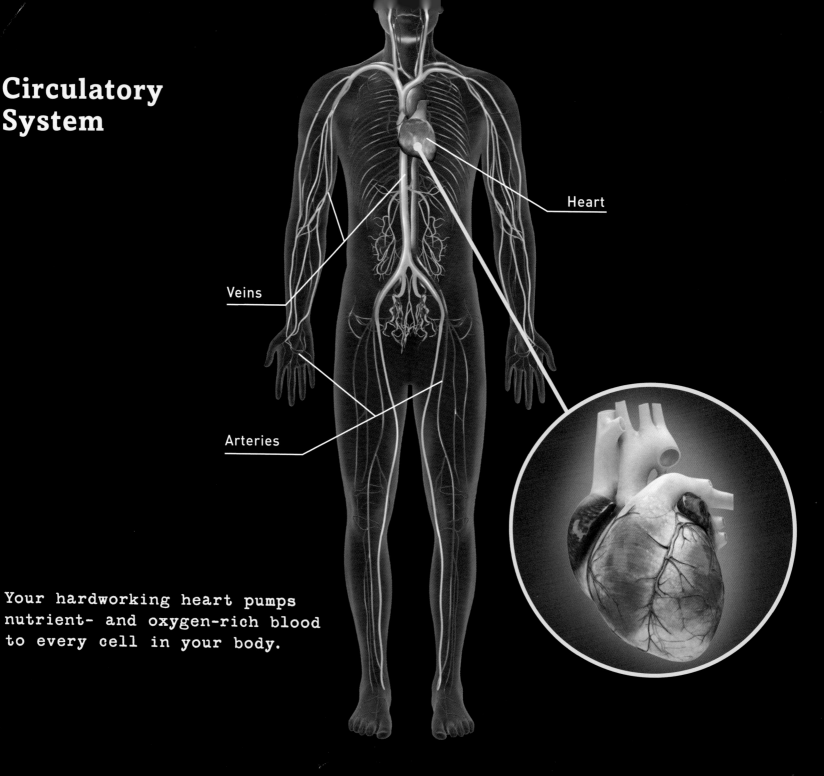

Heart

Veins

Arteries

Your hardworking heart pumps nutrient- and oxygen-rich blood to every cell in your body.

Why does my heart pump blood?

Your heart is a muscle the size of your fist. It beats about eighty times a minute, day and night, year after year. During your lifetime, your heart will beat about three billion times. And it will pump about 100 million gallons (380 million L) of blood through three kinds of tubes, or vessels, called arteries, capillaries, and veins. But why? Why is pumping blood so important?

Your blood is like an express-mail carrier. It makes pickups and deliveries all day long. Because most of the cells in your body can't move, they depend on blood. Blood brings your cells all the raw materials they need to function. What supplies do your cells need the most? Nutrients and oxygen.

As blood flows past your stomach and small intestines, it picks up nutrients. And as it flows around the alveolar sacs in your lungs, it collects oxygen. At the same time, your blood drops off carbon dioxide, so it can be removed from your body.

You have 60,000 miles of arteries, capillaries, and veins in your body. As blood travels through them, it delivers oxygen, nutrients, and other materials to your cells. Inside your cells, oxygen mixes with a sugary nutrient called glucose. What's the result of this important chemical reaction? All the energy your body needs to live and grow and move.

How does my body protect me?

Your skin is like a suit of armor. It keeps out dirt, dust, smoke, and germs. But your skin doesn't cover your entire body. Germs and other invaders can sneak in through your nose, mouth, ears, and eyes. They can enter through cuts, too. Luckily, your body has lots of ways to fight these pesky pests.

Tears wash germs out of your eyes. Earwax traps anything that flies, floats, or crawls into your ears. Nose hairs, snot, sneezing, and coughing protect your nose and lungs. Spit keeps your mouth clean.

If you eat food with harmful germs, vomiting and diarrhea can get them out of your body in a hurry. Bleeding gets rid of germs that sneak in through cuts and scrapes. All these battling bodyguards stop millions of germs before they make you sick, but they can't stop all the tiny trespassers. That's why it's a good thing you have white blood cells (WBCs).

When you get a cut, WBCs rush to the scene. Some gobble up bits of dirt. Others attack germs in the wound. When WBCs detect germs that cause colds or the flu or just about any other illness you can think of, they fight the invaders to the death.

Sometimes WBCs lose a battle, but that's OK. Your body makes ten billion new WBCs every day. Eventually, these dutiful defenders defeat the germs.

From battling germs and delivering nutrients to sensing danger and moving you from place to place, your amazing body is perfectly designed to help you survive in the world.

White blood cells surround a dangerous cancer cell and attack it.

The Human Body

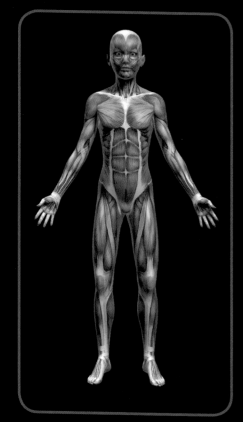

Muscular system

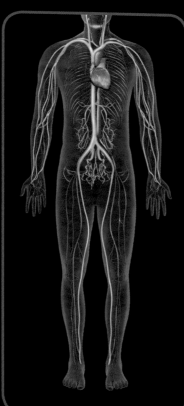

Circulatory system

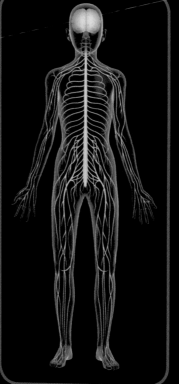

Nervous system

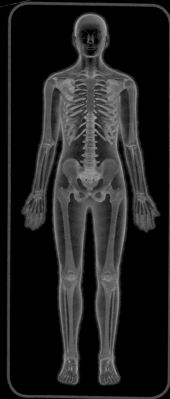

Skeletal system

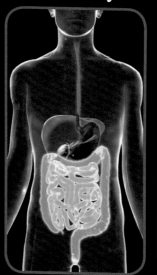

Digestive system

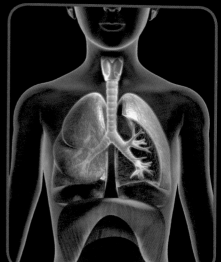

Respiratory system

FIND OUT MORE

Books to Read

Macaulay, David. *The Way We Work: Getting to Know the Amazing Human Body*. Boston, MA: Houghton Mifflin, 2008.

Macnair, Patricia. *Everything You Need to Know about the Human Body*. New York: Kingfisher, 2011.

Nye, Bill. *Great Big Book of Tiny Germs*. New York: Hyperion, 2005.

Rotner, Shelly and David A. White. *Body Actions*. New York: Holiday House, 2012.

Seuling, Barbara. *Your Skin Weighs More Than Your Brain and Other Freaky Facts about Your Skin, Skeleton, and Other Body Parts*. Mankato, MN: Picture Window Books, 2008.

Simon, Seymour. *Guts: Our Digestive System*. New York: HarperCollins, 2005.

Solway, Andrew. *The Respiratory System*. Chicago: World Book, Inc., 2007.

Stewart, Melissa. *Germ Wars: The Secrets of Protecting Your Body*. Tarrytown, NY: Benchmark Books, 2011.

———. *Moving and Grooving: The Secrets of Muscles and Bones*. Tarrytown, NY: Benchmark Books, 2011.

———. *Pump It Up!: The Secrets of the Heart and Blood*. Tarrytown, NY: Benchmark Books, 2010.

———. *The Skin You're In: The Secrets of Skin*. Tarrytown, NY: Benchmark Books, 2010.

———. *You've Got Nerve: The Secrets of the Brain and Nerves*. Tarrytown, NY: Benchmark Books, 2011.

Websites to Visit

GET BODY SMART
This site contains text and diagrams that give a complete overview of your body systems. It includes the nervous system, respiratory system, skeletal system, muscular system, and more.
http://www.getbodysmart.com

THE GIANT HEART
A great overview of the heart and its workings.
http://www.fi.edu/biosci/index.html

KIDS HEALTH
Answers to just about any question you might have about your body and keeping it healthy.
http://kidshealth.org/kid/

NEUROSCIENCE FOR KIDS
This site has simple, clear descriptions and explanations of the parts of the brain and nervous system and how they work.
http://faculty.washington.edu/chudler/introb.html

THAT EXPLAINS IT!
All kinds of interesting information about the human body and more.
http://www.coolquiz.com/trivia/explain/

For bibliography and free activities visit: http://www.sterlingpublishing.com/kids/good-question

INDEX